THE MOUNTIE AND MY MIND

BREAKING THE SILENCE

TIM R BEDARD

The Mountie and my Mind
Copyright © 2024 by Tim R Bedard

All rights reserved. No part of this publication may be reproduced, distributed, or transmitted in any form or by any means, including photocopying, recording, or other electronic or mechanical methods, without the prior written permission of the author, except in the case of brief quotations embodied in critical reviews and certain other non-commercial uses permitted by copyright law.

Tellwell Talent
www.tellwell.ca

ISBN
978-1-77941-923-1 (Hardcover)
978-1-77941-922-4 (Paperback)
978-1-77941-924-8 (eBook)

TABLE OF CONTENTS

Dedication v
About the Author vii
Acknowledgment ix
Introduction xi
Chapter 1   How it happened 1
Chapter 2   Trail of mittens 19
Chapter 3   Shotgun 22
Chapter 4   Homebrew 24
Chapter 5   Shots fired 26
Chapter 6   Please, listen to me. 28
Chapter 7   Up in flames 31
Chapter 8   Gas sniffers 32
Chapter 9   You're my backup? 33
Chapter 10   Out of gas 35
Chapter 11   The La Bamba plane 39
Chapter 12   It's now a step side. 40
Chapter 13   Dogs 42
Chapter 14   Patch over and time to move 46
Chapter 15   Chili 49
Chapter 16   Machete 51
Chapter 17   The switch 53
Chapter 18   Fight at Home Depot 55
Chapter 19   Spiderman 57
Chapter 20   Gerald 59
Chapter 21   I'll hold your hand. 60
Chapter 22   The Depot Days 62
Conclusion 79

Dedication

This book is dedicated to my son, Dawson; you have witnessed your father struggle with his mental health since a very young age, yet you were always understanding and compassionate. In my darkest times, you were my light and my reason for still staying on this earth. I love you.

About the Author

Tim Bedard, a native of the small, French town of Girouxville in northern Alberta, Canada, was raised amidst the rugged landscapes of the region. Currently residing in Qualicum Beach, nestled on scenic Vancouver Island in British Columbia, Tim shares his home with his son, his faithful cat, and his service dog, Hazel. Driven by a desire to inspire and connect with others, Tim aims to share his personal narrative to illuminate the path of resilience and solidarity, affirming that "no one walks alone".

Acknowledgment

I am profoundly grateful to the countless individuals who have stood by me unwaveringly throughout my journey with mental health challenges and addiction. Your steadfast support and belief in me, even during the darkest of times, have been nothing short of life-saving. To all the healthcare providers who have been part of my journey, your care and compassion have made a significant difference in my life. I am deeply thankful to my parents for their enduring love and strength, despite witnessing their son's struggles. And to my son, your presence has been my greatest motivation for recovery. After years of navigating through darkness, I am finally beginning to see the glimmer of light ahead. This journey has reaffirmed that I am not alone.

Introduction

It was October 23, 2006, and at the age of 26 years old, I just graduated from the Royal Canadian Mounted Police (RCMP) Cadet Training Program as a member of a First Nations police service (Tribal Police). My first posting was where I did six months side by side with the RCMP. Our uniforms were black with a red stripe down the sides of our pants. That year, I was stationed in an isolated and remote post in Northern Alberta. One of the communities that I policed was only accessible by plane, barge, or winter road. In August 2009, did a lateral transfer into the RCMP.

That is when the RCMP absorbed my three years of service with the Tribal Police, and I took no additional training. Just a new uniform and badge. Prior to being a police officer, I was a correctional officer for three years and before that did various security jobs. It was from 2003 to 2006 that I put myself through post-secondary school at MacEwan University in Edmonton, Alberta. That is where I received a certificate in Aboriginal Police Studies and a diploma in Police Studies. After completion of my studies, I was hired by two different police agencies which included me passing all background checks with additional mental health exams and assessments. It was very rewarding work that I loved, and I was considered a top performer by superiors, including my peers.

My family roots and background that I identify with are French Canadian/Metis. I have been diagnosed with severe post traumatic stress disorder (PTSD), major depressive disorder, and general anxiety disorder because of my service with the RCMP. In April of 2019, I had to leave the RCMP and career that I loved due to my disabilities that happened while serving my country. I'm sharing my personal story and experiences to help other RCMP members and/or any first responders that might be going through the same thing so they can come forward to get the help they need before it's too late. My other objective is to try and improve the current support systems that are unfortunately failing at times or have short falls. I want to create positive changes towards mental health stigmas to help all first responders through education and speaking publicly with firsthand experiences that I have gone through.

CHAPTER 1

How it happened

It's strange looking back now, but I never wanted to be a police officer when I was growing up. It wasn't until I was in my early 20's that I heard the calling, and that's when I knew that this was what I was supposed to do with my life. It was to help people and give back to my community and country. I did everything that I could do to increase my chances for trying to enter the RCMP. I started working security jobs, and in 2003 began my first of three years at MacEwan University in Edmonton, Alberta. During this time, I was a correctional officer at the Fort Saskatchewan Correctional Centre. I oversaw a 60-man open unit, along with a case worker.

In May of 2006, I graduated from MacEwan University with a certificate in Aboriginal Police Studies and a two-year diploma in Police Studies. After graduation, I was accepted into the Cadet Training Program at the RCMP "Depot" Division in Regina, Saskatchewan, as a member of a Tribal Police Service. At that moment, it was probably one of the best times of my life. To this day, I still laugh with some of my troopmates about the shenanigans that occurred there. On October 23, 2006, I graduated from the academy and off to Northern Alberta I went.

The Tribal Police Service I worked with had three constables, one corporal, and a chief of police that was a borrowed corporal from the RCMP. Just as it was when I was in Depot, I worked side by side with the RCMP in their detachment. We went on calls together most of the time when a family fight complaint would come in and other general duty work that needed to be done. My patrol area covered several First Nation communities. One community, on the other hand, was only accessible by air, barge, or winter road. Most people, including children, were still speaking Cree as a primary language there.

I learned pretty quickly how to say "white guy, police" and other useful words, including swear words. As this was an isolated community, there were only three constables for a population of 1753: One for dayshift, one for night shift, and one on days off. We basically worked alone and sometimes you were the only one in the community as the other two flew out to court for the day.

My first few weeks on the job was a whirlwind. The first dead body I had to put in a body bag, was the brother of my high-school girlfriend. I also faced a child's death for the first time. A young five-year-old boy was eaten in one of the communities by at least five dogs.

My trainer didn't want me to see the little boy as he was covered under a blanket on the cold winter road with half of his face eaten. My job was to retrace his steps and retrieve his trail of winter gear. I especially remember his mittens and was exposed to a lot during that posting. I learned a lot working for the Tribal Police and in August of 2009, I had enough education and experience to be sworn in as a member of the Royal Canadian Mounted Police. With my first fiancée and stepson, we packed our bags and were off to "E" Division, in British Columbia. This was another First Nation community in the northern part of the province. It was a six-member detachment and a limited duration post.

I dealt with many traumatic calls on my own during this time. There were two calls that I remember and is when I started noticing, afterwards, that I was showing signs of Post Traumatic Stress Disorder but didn't know it. During one incident, I arrested a male who was intoxicated and in a domestic dispute. I was alone and got into a wrestling match with him on the porch of his home. During the scuffle, he kicked me and hit me in the groin barely missing my testicles. Even while handcuffed, that client was also able to take a tug on my service pistol.

The second incident was after I got into another wrestling match. This time it was in the ditch with a man that was over six feet tall, and I am five foot and six inches. We got a call of an intoxicated male wandering the street. Keep in mind that it was 3 a.m. and it was winter in Northern British Columbia. I arrived on scene and found the intoxicated male stumbling down the road. I activated my emergency lights and got out of my vehicle. That's when I attempted to arrest the male for being intoxicated in public, and the fight was on. He pulled away from me and we both fell into the ditch.

It was a deep ditch full of snow. Immediately, I pressed my 10-33 button—officer in distress—and I didn't know if it went through prior to my radio mic falling off. So, here I was, and this large guy was on top of me at one point and we were dancing in the ditch. I looked up at one point and saw his friend watching us. That's when I thought to myself, shit, he's going to jump in. I had no idea if I was going to make it out of this one. It turned out my emergency call for help did go through and dispatch was able to hear the commotion. Dispatch was able to call backup, who threw on his duty belt and vest and came and found me still struggling. I can't tell you how long this all went on, but it felt like forever. We were able to get the male under control and transport him to the detachment jail cell.

It was the next week that I pulled someone over for an impaired investigation when he said to me "I'm not going to hurt you." This guy was nice and not a threat to me at all. Then, I looked down at my hands and they were shaking. The shaking continued and people I would deal with would make comments about my shaking. Eventually, I just said that I was diabetic and needed to eat. That was a total lie, but that's how I coped with it.

There were so many traumatic events that I had dealt with on my own, just like the others; a suicide by hanging, where I was alone and had to cut him down and commenced CPR while using a grocery bag to cover his mouth. I attended a call on my own where I could have had my head chopped off. Then there was having to do the HIV cocktail because I was exposed to blood, and then waiting six months to find out if you contracted HIV. The HIV cocktail therapy refers to a combination of antiretroviral drugs used to treat HIV infection. These cocktails typically consist of a combination of different medications to target the virus in various ways, helping to control its replication and progression.

It was 2010, and I was really starting to notice changes with me. I had no idea what was going on. Post Traumatic Stress Disorder wasn't talked about or known yet in my career. But here I was having my life fall apart, and I had no clue who this demon was that was doing it. The us-versus-them mentality started to settle in as my paranoia began. I began getting lost going to calls. My head became foggy. Then, I began isolating myself and I didn't want my fiancée talking to the locals or making friends. I started to become emotionally abusive towards my fiancée. There were so many signs when I look back, that I was clearly starting to fall apart. I began to avoid pulling people over for simple traffic infractions because of my anxiety and fear of confrontation. I would snap on a moment's notice and rage would build inside of me. My home life was falling apart. I began to use food to cope. My fiancée, now pregnant, and I would argue all the time, but I continued onward the best I could.

In December of 2010 my son was born. It was two months later that my fiancée would leave me with our son to go live on Vancouver Island. I requested a transfer but had to wait. I missed out on a lot of my son's precious moments, even missed the birth. I was on parental leave for all this time, alone, sitting in my house up north. It's a good thing that I didn't drink as things would have become worse.

At that time, I remember spending many nights sitting in my closet crying and wondering what was going on with my life. Being an hour and a half away from the city centre, I was stuck. I should have had the RCMP help me from the beginning of my mental health deterioration, but I was missed. In July of 2011, I officially transferred to a detachment towards the middle region of Vancouver Island. This is the biggest detachment on the island with over 200-plus members. This is also where everything exploded for me, and where my career ended eight years later.

My time there was filled with violence towards me. It was like people were attracted to me just to follow through with violent acts. My first week involved me getting kicked in the groin, again, while arresting someone on a Sunday morning at Home Depot in the plumbing aisle. I fell victim to numerous assaults and threats. Unfortunately, I managed to accumulate being on our police information systems 14 times as a victim of various criminal acts towards me. Those were the big ones that I felt needed to be recorded. No matter what I did, people wanted to fight me. When looking back on things now, I was spiraling out of control.

The us-versus-them mentality caused me to have no friends outside of work. If you were not a cop, I wasn't going to talk to you as you couldn't be trusted. The paranoid mentality also started and I began locking myself in my house on days off. People tell me now that I used to go to simple calls, such as a shoplifter, and be jacked right up. It was a constant adrenal dump. I also continued to eat my feelings and I weighed up to 242 lbs. It was around the fall of 2011 that I went to my family doctor and told him about the experiences I was having. He didn't understand and just told me I needed counseling, so I started seeing a psychologist.

Most of my sessions were focused on my separation from my spouse and loss of a family. We touched a little bit on my now known issues, but it was never dug into or officially diagnosed yet. PTSD was only discovered years later, but by that time it was too late. It was in this time frame as well that I went to the Pacific Regional Training Centre in Chilliwack to recertify in various steps, like firearms, use of force, etc.

They gave me a full medical by the RCMP doctor, and I told him about the experiences that I was having. The doctor just asked if I was seeing someone and that was it. I was never spoken to about PTSD or mental illness. So, I continued to work and was flying more and more off the handle. Then I began to snap at people at the drop of a hat. Some supervisors would tell me to leave the jail cell block if I came down to assist a prisoner, as people would be attracted to fight me. My sleep was also a complete disaster. The fights continued.

On November 13, 2013, I arrested a female on a Mental Health Act complaint. The female was suicidal and she was brought to the hospital to be assessed in the psychiatric ward. It was here that a nurse and I got into a confrontation. The nurse had demanded that the handcuffs come off the female. However, she had not been searched thoroughly by me at the time, so I disagreed with the nurse. I also began to shake. I would shake to the point where I could not take any notes in my notebook. I remember this because I had tried and the security guard saw this and laughed at me. I began to shake severely. Against my own intuition, I took the handcuffs off the female without her being searched. The nurse also made a public complaint against me. The next nightshift I brought another patient into the psych ward, and I recall the nurses rolling their eyes at me.

It was shortly after this that I had a meeting with my staff sergeant. This staff sergeant had investigated me for a previous public complaint against me a few years prior, which had been deemed unfounded. He had worked in professional standards. During the meeting he brought that up to remind me. It was at this time that he compared me to a former co-worker of his that he used to work with. He explained that his co-worker had been in the Canadian Forces and was now a member of the RCMP. This person was described by the staff sergeant to be known to walk around town like he was still in a war zone. I was told that this is what I reminded him of. Again, nothing about PTSD was brought up. Then, I used my holiday time to take a month off work and clear my head.

In January of 2014, I went back to work. I did not know that soon on the horizon I would get into an incident that would eventually be the straw that broke the camel's back. The hypervigilance, violence, being spit into my mouth, and exposed to another round of HIV cocktail all continued. Everything was out of control. Furthermore, the nurses that made a complaint against me came to the office to have a meeting with me and the staff sergeant. During the meeting, the nurses explained that they feared me because I had been shaking. They were also concerned about the safety of the public. I finished the meeting, made my amends, and continued to work. Things just got worse, and I was accumulating more entries on police information systems as a victim. Use of force reports piled up and more public complaints about me came rolling in. There was supposed to be a flagging system in place for members to warn upper management that a person may need help. This system would be set off if you had a certain number of use-of-force reports, entries on police information systems, and public complaints. Unfortunately, I was missed and continued to work on the road as a general duty constable until the fateful morning of June 25, 2014.

It was early morning, about 5 a.m., when a suspect was arrested for stealing a car from a neighboring community. I was about to finish my shift, but I decided to head down to the jail cell area to help another constable with the process of getting the suspect settled in his jail cell. The now prisoner had become aggressive at this time and refused to take the string out of his shorts. RCMP protocols state that a prisoner cannot be left with a string, as there is a danger of self-strangulation with it. We called a supervisor and updated her on the circumstances about him refusing to take the string out. It was insisted by my supervisor that the string must come out. I approached his jail cell and made my first mistake by opening the cell door to talk to him. Then, I made my second mistake by entering his cell with my hands by my side. I asked him politely to take the string out of his shorts, as there would be seven of us coming down to do it if he didn't comply. It was at this point that I was punched in the side of the head.

What I saw in my head and what I watched on the security cameras afterwards were two separate things. I snapped into a different state of mind: survival. I was going home at the end of my shift. In my head I rushed the prisoner to the back bunk of the cell to which he fell on his back. Then I struck him twice in the head with a closed fist. I stopped and looked at my partner who had rushed to see the commotion. My partner was now trying to subdue the prisoner's legs. The prisoner and I then fell to the floor to which I delivered another two or three punches to the head. It was at this point that several members entered the jail cell and took over. I left the cell and "woke up," not really understanding what happened. Then I realized that I had blood on my face. I looked at the prisoner and saw what I did. It was at that point that I knew I needed a lawyer.

It was later that I was able to view the jail cell block footage with my psychologist. On video you saw me enter the jail cell with my hands down and talking to the prisoner. I then get punched in the head to which you see my head twist over my right shoulder. Then I watched myself rush the prisoner to the back of the bunk and began striking him in the head. My partner had entered the cell and was assisting to get the prisoner under control. The prisoner and I fell on the floor to which I was still striking the prisoner in the head. The final two blows that ruined me were when the prisoner was covering his face with his hands. In approximately 12 seconds, that prisoner was punched in the head by me approximately 11 times.

I left the cell area in shock, cleaned up and headed to my police cruiser which was parked in the parking lot and texted a friend to talk to me. After we spoke, I began writing my report. It was a short time later that I observed an ambulance come out of the prisoner intake lobby to which they were bringing the prisoner to the hospital. I had made a bloody mess of his face and broke his nose. Then, I realized that I injured my right hand punching him in the head, so I finished my report, went off shift, and went directly to the hospital to have my hand checked out. After the hospital I went home, tried to sleep, and got updates about the prisoner who had been in the hospital. It was in the afternoon that I found out that the Independent Investigations Office was investigating me for use of force. I was off work for four days and as a single dad I was trying to keep it together for my son. The Independent Investigations Office (IIO) is an independent civilian-led agency responsible for conducting investigations into incidents involving serious harm or death that may have resulted from the actions of police officers. It operates at arm's length from the police to ensure transparency and accountability in the investigation process. The IIO investigates these incidents to determine whether any officer may have committed an offense and, if so, forwards the findings to Crown Counsel for consideration of charges.

Upon my return to work, I was brought up to the corner office and served code of conduct documents by the superintendent. I was told that he looked at my file and saw no reason to suspend me, and I was back on the road working for two days and two nights. Despite going through all of this, I had no debriefing. In fact, I never had one debriefing in my career with the RCMP. The only debrief I had was after the child got eaten by dogs up north at the start of my career, and that was with the Tribal Police. I tried to work but anxiety took over. I almost vomited arresting someone, and I was crashing mentally. At some point during these four days, I spoke with my staff sergeant who told me that I "looked like a Metis warrior in the cell block with my haircut." I couldn't discern his intentions behind telling this or the significance of his statement. As a Metis person, I've often questioned what society expects someone of my background to look like. His comment felt offensive and left me with further mental confusion to my already fragile state. Furthermore, I was now seeing things in my head and losing control of my mind.

On July 11, 2014, I was on my days off and isolating myself in my home. I read about the investigation surrounding me and it was enough to make me have a mental breakdown. I drove myself to the hospital, told the staff my story, and demanded that somebody help me. It was at that point, four years after I started reaching out for help, that someone listened to me. I was written off work pending my psychologist appointment. I had spoken with a co-worker during this time who told me to have my psychologist test specifically for Post Traumatic Stress Disorder.

A test was done and after a few days the results came back as suspected. I was diagnosed with Post Traumatic Stress Disorder. My psychologist wrote me off work pending further treatment. I brought my paperwork to my staff sergeant and told him that I had good news and bad news. The good news was that they finally found out what was wrong with me. The bad news was that I was going to be off work for a while. It was silent for a bit, and I noticed my staff sergeant's demeanor change. I asked him if he was mad, to which he stated no, but then proceeded to tell me that other people would now have to pick up the slack. To me, this felt like a guilt trip to get me back to work.

After many months away from work and working with my psychologist, I returned to desk duty at the office thinking I could handle it. However, my mind was gone and I had meltdowns in the office, which led to being pulled from my watch that I felt I had a connection with. I was working in the office with others, but feeling alone at the same time. Eventually, it got so bad that I disconnected my doorbell at home and put up no trespassing signs in my yard. I even contemplated building a fence around my entire home to shield me from the outside world.

It was in February of 2015 that I was charged criminally for assault causing bodily harm for the jail cell block incident that occurred in July 2014. I was devastated. I couldn't explain the discrepancy between what I remembered in my head and what was on the video of that night. My name and face were plastered all over the media, online, and I had a television camera shoved in my face as I walked to and from the courthouse for my appearances. This all dragged on until December 15,2015, when I was given a conditional discharge and put on probation for a year. A coworker tried to fingerprint me, but I ended up fingerprinting myself as they were my friend and too upset to do it. I had my criminal photo taken by police and by probation. I was humiliated, and now knew what it felt like to be on the other side of the law. I remember during my sentencing that the judge told me that I was a good cop, and it served no purpose that I have a criminal record. The judge also stated that I had reasons to fear for my safety and my son's safety.

My life was ruined from this point onward. I was using food to cope and to the point that I would eat so much I would vomit and keep on eating. Eating numbed the pain. I was crying for no reason, seeing fight scenes in my head, was paranoid in public, developed a stutter, and had memory loss and suicidal thoughts. It felt like I was in full-blown mental breakdown, but I continued to work.

I slowly worked at jobs in the office, all while trying to keep it together, and I eventually got back on D-Watch as the detachment constable. Ironically, part of my job was back in the jail cell block processing prisoners. It felt like I finally had some supervisors that understood me—I did have a handful during my time that helped me out. I was still having a hard time, though, and having flashbacks in the cell block, seeing people punch me in the head when I would fingerprint them.

My friend, a female sergeant that didn't put up with bullshit, retired and I had a hard time with it as she was my anchor. Another sergeant on my watch, that understood me, transferred and the only person I had left was my new staff sergeant. He was genuine and understood me as well. One night, I had a meltdown in the detachment after someone raised their voice at me. I tried to tell a corporal what was going on and I couldn't talk, I just stuttered. Then I sat in the supervisor's office by myself and cried until I could talk. No one checked in with me.

On February 20, 2017, I was written off work again by my psychologist because I couldn't handle it. I had given it my best shot, but my duties at work were being pushed and no one understood me anymore. During that time, I was going on my second family trial in family court with my first fiancée. I couldn't handle anything and was off work for a month, until March 17, 2017. I didn't receive one phone call or message from any of my supervisors to see if I was okay. I could have hung myself and no one would have cared. I was starting to have enough of my situation and contemplated taking my life just to get some peace. There was even a plan that I devised where I would leave a note on the front door of my home requesting that certain members from the local detachment do not enter the home as I was personal friends with them. My plan was that I would go into the bathtub and slit my wrists. This way it would be clean and I would just bleed out into the drain.

Eventually, I went back to work and tried again, but I couldn't do anything by myself as my anxiety was too much. I had to get others to assist me when I was in the jail cell block and I felt stupid asking for help. I could tell that people were starting to get annoyed with me and the assistance that was needed. Things didn't improve from there.

It was August of 2017 that my son was lying awake in bed with me. I fell asleep and had a night terror. I woke up punching, and if my son would have been sitting up in bed, I would have punched him in the head. That was the last straw. My son had seen me at my worst at the young age of seven.

I yell like I have Tourette's. I can't handle noise and my son hears me stutter and sees me forget simple tasks. He had to walk on eggshells, and I had to explain to him that I had a brain injury from the bad things I saw and the things that happened to me being a policeman. It was after this that I had a talk with a co-worker who convinced me that I needed to seek help from the British Columbia Operational Stress Injury Clinic. I took his advice and demanded that health services send me there and that I wanted to see a psychiatrist who specializes in PTSD.

My final stint at work only lasted around two months before I had to pull the pin again. It was the end of September in 2017 and I was advised by a supervisor that my medical certificate had expired. This was enough to set me off into a spin.

A couple days after being signed off on a medical leave, I had a meeting with an inspector, my sergeant, and my staff sergeant. I was under the impression that when I returned to work, they would be able to find me a job that I could handle. One of my supervisors complained to the inspector that this was taking officers off the road to assist me. The supervisors had to send emails for me because I couldn't even handle that. I was told that this information was not being said to be hurtful, but that's what it felt like to me inside. The inspector spoke about other officers leaving the force and thriving and how I would always have good memories. Before I went home, my sergeant asked if I would like phone calls to check up on me. I stated yes, but unfortunately those phone calls never happened. The inspector also asked me if I had any suicidal thoughts. I lied and stated no because I feared the repercussions.

After that meeting, I went home because I felt sick, so sick that I held a knife to my wrist and imagined how easy it would be to slit my wrist to get relief. I also imagined sitting in my car and gassing myself, or I would make a handgun gesture with my hand and pretend to shoot myself.

Days passed by and I would just stay in bed in a state of depression hoping that someone would reach out to me. I would lay in bed wondering what was going on in my life and thinking how easy it would be just to end it all. I understood firsthand why other first responders with PTSD kill themselves. They want to feel relief. At the end of November 2017, after my first appointment with the psychiatrist at the Operational Stress Injury Clinic, I sent an email to the inspector and advised that I was still alive. Little did I know that in the background of all of this, a plan was being put in place to force me out of the RCMP due to my medical condition, plus the mental health issues that developed over the years being a police officer.

On January 18, 2018, I spoke with the inspector and advised that I would like to get back to work in the office doing something I could handle. I felt that I could be useful and could still contribute. That's when she told me that "we can't always get what we want" and reminded me that another option was to voluntarily release myself from the police force. Once again, I felt abandoned by people that I once trusted with my life and held to high regard.

In the week of May 6, 2018, I received a phone call out of the blue from the inspector and was told the disability manager was having meetings at the detachment with everyone that was on medical leave. I was told that it was not anything to worry about and was just to talk about my updated medical status. My psychiatrist had drafted a return-to-work schedule for me with restrictions to enable me to succeed. That's when I told the inspector that I had been cleared to go back to work two months ago and I hadn't heard anything.

On May 16th, 2018, at 8:30 a.m., I met with the inspector and disability manager from the RCMP. When I walked into the meeting, I did not know this was going to be the end of my career. During the meeting, they had to stop it three times to make sure I was okay. I had, in fact, seen black spots and the walls of the room were closing in. I was told it would be a good idea to start my disability claim, despite both of my doctors stating that I needed to stay there to succeed and for reasons that would affect my mental health. I was told that I didn't have to pack my locker then, but I chose to because I was done and I didn't want to come back to the detachment. Someone that I had no connection to was watching over my shoulder while I packed my locker belongings and then left the detachment.

October 23, 2006, I walked out of the RCMP training academy with a sense of pride and accomplishment. Then, on May 16, 2018, I packed my career into a cardboard box. At this point I was mentally destroyed. I was going to lose my career; a career that got me sick in the first place. Naturally, I was mad and sad at the same time.

On April 24, 2019, I officially medically retired from the RCMP. I had lost my career and my only known identity and had to start over while still dealing with my demons inside. It was a very rough road from that point on. Suicidal thoughts and acts, depression, rage, overeating, and numbness were all there. I was so bad that at one point I video called my now second ex-fiancée—we met in June of 2018—with a knife to my throat wanting to kill myself. I had also been running knives on my wrists. She didn't call the police out of fear it would push me over the edge. Instead, she called my father who came and calmed me down. At one point, I told myself that enough was enough and I asked Veterans Affairs Canada to send me to a trauma and recovery program at a treatment centre. They were able to help and sent me to a 49-day program.

It was during these 49 days that I had been sober for over a year. I had been granted medicinal marijuana to ease my mind. This worked well for a while until I began abusing it, like getting high at two in the afternoon when I didn't have my son. I began chasing a high wherever I could. It numbed the pain, and during my time at the treatment centre I went without it, but replaced it with more prescription medication.

I had met some awesome people at the program to which I still stay in contact with. Sadly, the program was not strong enough to overcome my demons. I did my 49 days and wanted to do a week more. That didn't happen. During my time there, I had constant suicidal thoughts to which I would get spoken to about regularly. I would yell emotionally abusive language to my fiancée over the phone. On two occasions I just flipped out. The first one was after being triggered by observing two people get into an argument. I began slamming chairs around, yelling and going after one of them.

I eventually was put in a choke hold by a friend in order to snap out of it. The second incident was on my 49th day when I got triggered by a counsellor and began yelling that I wanted to leave. Police were called on me this time, but were called off when I calmed down and began packing my items. It was later found out that the counsellor called me a cancer infecting other people and was glad I was gone. They also told people that I couldn't be helped. My fiancée came to pick me up and was told that there was nothing more they could do to help me. I went home and for a week I would cling on to my fiancée. Things continued to spiral, and it eventually affected my relationship again. I would yo-yo from months of being good to bad again. At some point, my fiancée would come over to my place (we hadn't moved in together yet) and told me to get out of bed, shave, and shower. My place would be a disaster. I would need help shopping and struggled with all my ups and downs. It was never ending, and still is not.

In September of 2021, my second fiancée left me because of my mental health. I had tried to come off medication and it did not turn out well, eventually ruining my relationship. I remind myself that I passed two psychological background checks and tests by two different police agencies and cleared them both. So, at one point I was healthy.

My mind has subjected me to a series of challenges: paranoia in public spaces, vivid but unreal fights playing out in my head, overeating to numb emotional pain, neglecting hygiene and spending days in bed, experiencing stuttering and memory lapses, battling flashbacks, mood swings, and marijuana addiction. I've also wrestled with rage outbursts and seizures due to medication side effects, alongside suspicion towards others and Tourette-like outbursts. Triggered easily, I oscillate between tears and aggression, while anxiety often leaves me mentally spinning. At times, passive suicidal thoughts linger and I struggle to control my emotions, sometimes becoming emotionally abusive. Detaching from reality, I find it difficult to empathize with others' needs. Additionally, I grapple with weight issues and a heightened startle response. I've been in the care of a psychiatrist, psychologist, counselor, went through two occupational therapists, and had a case manager through Veterans Affairs Canada.

My journey with mental illness has been tough. The purpose of sharing some of my story is to hopefully help someone who may be needing to read this. I've been through hell and back and I am still here. So, whatever you do, do not give up.

Graduation from RCMP Training Academy as a member of the Tribal Police in October 23rd, 2006

Chapter 2

Trail of mittens

It was November 16, 2006, at approximately 5:30 pm. I was seven days shy of my first month into policing, and my recruit field trainer and I were enroute to one of the communities when that call came in. A sudden death involving a child. Further information provided that he had been mauled by stray dogs that were roaming the community. Lights and sirens were put on and we raced to the community about 30 minutes away. My heart was pounding, not knowing really what to expect. This would be the first death of a child that I would deal with in my 13-year career of policing.

I remember arriving on scene and getting out of the patrol vehicle. It was cold, snowing, and the cold air slapped me right in the face. The little boy, five years old, was lying on the frozen ground covered with a blanket and surrounded by three community members. My training officer, Scott, took charge of the scene and I was in charge of the evidence and taking photographs. Scott approached the boy and I was behind him. He lifted the blanket and noticed that the boy had half of his face chewed off, as if the dogs had been hungry, and the boy was the prey. Scott didn't let me see the little boy and I was okay with that.

With some direction from Scott, I began retracing this little boy's steps in the snow, eventually finding a trail of mittens and a toque that had been left by a house. I can remember his small footprints in the snow and picking up the items as I walked. I took photos of the scene before I touched anything and one by one, seized the items and put them into exhibit bags.

We got information that the two dogs that were responsible for the death of this innocent child were chained up in someone's yard. I got further direction from Scott and attended a residence to take a statement from someone that had been a witness. With the statement taken, my next step was to seize the dogs. The dogs were two rottweilers and were loaded into the rear of my police vehicle. I then proceeded to take paper bags and seize the dogs' fecal matter.

With the dogs in my truck, I transported them to the veterinary clinic where I updated the veterinarian on the investigation and what needed to be done. They were eventually euthanized. During the transport, the dogs had seemed harmless. They didn't bark or act aggressive.

It was upsetting for me to find out later that this was the second child in the area to be killed by stray dogs. I don't remember much else about the incident, but for some reason I can still remember the smell of the dog feces that were in the paper bags and the fact that I placed them in the shed at the detachment. This would be a day that I would like to forget, but it's one of many stories that stay locked in my mind.

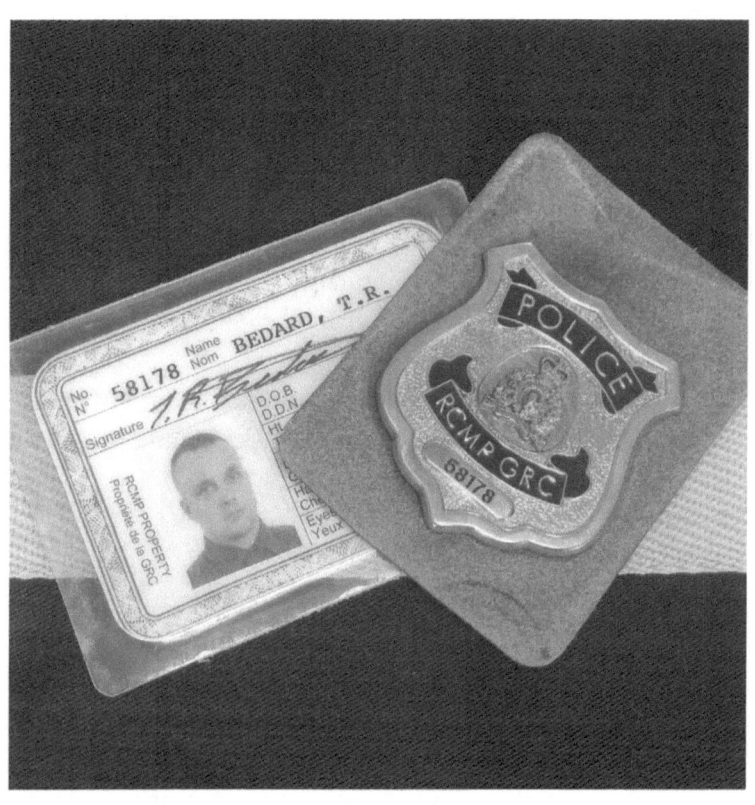

My Badge, Police Identification and Uniform Pants

Chapter 3

Shotgun

I remember that it was the beginning of the evening shift. It was calm and sunny and dry. Dust would float in the air as vehicles and quads would drive by the detachment. I was working alone as the dayshift had just ended. Then the call came in; it was a fight between a mother and son. Information provided that there was some sort of assault and the son had taken off with his mom in the car and a shotgun.

I had to make call out for the dayshift. Gilbert, my backup officer, was called. He got his uniform back on and came to the detachment where we gave the corporal a call to update him on the situation.

We had a choice where we could wait for the emergency response team to come from Edmonton, which in turn had a few factors that came into play. Edmonton was in the lower part of Northern Alberta and we were at the northern tip and they would have had to wait until daybreak to fly into the community. Or, we could go handle this situation ourselves, just the two of us.

Once on patrol, we went looking for a beat-up, old red Chevy. It didn't take us long to find the truck parked outside of a residence—mind you, the area wasn't very big. We parked far away from the house and updated police dispatch of what we were about to do. Police dispatch could be heard pretty good in the truck but not so much on the radios that were still in use from the time of Expo 86. You would have to wave the radio in the air like you were trying to flag down an airplane to get any reception.

We took a good look at the house, picturing worse case scenarios and finding plans of escape and other avenues. It was just the two of us and we had no clue what we were about to get into. Could this be another headline in the news? "Two cops dead in a shootout in Northern Alberta" The thought of this was a possibility. We approached the house carefully with our sidearms out at the low ready and took a peek in one of the bedroom windows. The window had been covered by a blanket but was open just enough to see inside the bedroom.

Gilbert approached first while I was right behind him. He told me that our suspect was in there sleeping on the bed, which was a mattress on the floor. Next to the door of the bedroom was the shotgun. Well shit, here we go, I thought.

I went first into the house, slowly opening the door. My heart was pounding. This guy could have heard us and was now waiting on the other side ready to blast us. We slowly made our way in, with Gilbert right behind me. The house opened right up into a big living room. Straight ahead was the kitchen and on the left was a hallway leading to the room which was at the end. Gilbert and I decided that I would enter the room and immediately seize the shotgun while Gilbert would apprehend the suspect. That's if everything worked out okay. So, we went down the hallway towards the room on the left with the door closed. That walk felt like an eternity. I could feel my heart pounding out of my chest and imagined the suspect coming out of and shooting us. We got to the end and I opened the door. The suspect was still on the bed and the shotgun was standing up against the door. I quickly seized the shotgun while Gilbert hopped on the bed and arrested the suspect.

Chapter 4

Homebrew

Addiction, it can happen to anyone if the circumstances are right, myself included. As I mentioned before, I have an addiction problem with marijuana. Something that was used properly for medical reasons turned into a blur with me chasing a high everyday in order to get out of my head. Homebrew was the "drug of choice" for some people where I was stationed. What was homebrew? Homebrew was a mix of dog food and yeast, which people would let ferment into a white milky colour to drink. It stunk to high heaven. It was not uncommon that we would go into a house and find adults huddled around an old oil can with a garbage bag in it as a liner. In the garbage bag was homebrew, some with dog food still floating around in it. People would be pissed just scooping up cups full of the stuff and chugging it. This stuff was poisonous and you could see it come out of people's faces. When dealing with someone, you would instantly know if they were a consumer of homebrew as their faces would puffy and ooze yeast sweat, if that makes any sense—I have no other way to describe it. And holy Christ, did it ever stink. Once you would get some on your uniform that would be it; it was time to change. There was no way you could finish a shift smelling like that.

People would get severely intoxicated on this stuff. You would pull someone over and instead of asking them, "How many drinks have you had tonight?" you would say, "How many cups have you had?" Addiction is horrible and people would go to great lengths to fulfill those needs.

And seeing someone go through DTs (Delirium Tremens, a life-threatening form of alcohol withdrawal that have symptoms such as shaking, confusion and hallucinations) was horrible. We would end up getting everyone assessed either at the nursing station or have the nurses come to the detachment to check the prisoner out. A person would usually start going through DTs once they had been staying for a while in jail with us, usually because a judge had ordered them to stay in custody until trial.

One time, I was walking into the detachment and someone going through DTs from homebrew came up to me with a straight face and asked me to shoot him. Needless to say, he was arrested on the spot under the Mental Health Act.

Chapter 5

Shots fired

During an evening shift in the fall, it was dark and calm and I had my windows open as I usually did while on slow patrol in the community. I kept my windows rolled down so I could better hear what was going on outside. I was driving by a local problem house when I heard KABOOM! I nearly shit my pants. Was I being shot at, I wondered? I stopped my police vehicle and hunched down inside so I could barely see over my steering wheel. I radioed police dispatch and told them that I heard a shotgun blast and it was quite close, and I didn't know if I was getting shot so to call out my backup.

My adrenaline was going and I had a feeling where the shotgun blast was coming from. Contrary to my training, and I still don't know why I did this, I drove half way up towards the house with my lights off and got on the loudspeaker. "Henry!" I yelled. "If that's you shooting off rounds from your front porch, flicker your porch lights!" What the fuck did I just say, I thought to myself. Henry was a nice guy and we always dealt with him when he was intoxicated. I guess this was my way to try and deescalate the situation. You see, everybody had a gun in the community. The last thing I wanted to do was get into a shootout.

I didn't get a response from Henry and I waited for my backup to arrive so we could make a plan. Backup arrived shortly and we decided to approach the house after carefully weighing our options. Henry had gone back into the house at this point and all the lights were on. We got police dispatch to call into the house and confirmed that Henry had shot a round off the porch of his house. We approached the house with one police vehicle, lights off and using it as a shield. We got on the loudspeaker and called Henry out of the house. Henry eventually came out; he was clearly intoxicated. We spoke with him for a while until we saw our opportunity when Henry started walking down the stairs. Henry was quickly put into cuffs. Now that Henry was safe, searched and placed in the back of the police vehicle, our focus was getting that shotgun. Usually, a search warrant would be needed to get into the house from this point but it was either Henry or a family member that invited us in. The shotgun was found in plain view in the foyer and we seized it. In the end no one was hurt. Henry was put in jail for his safety until he was sober in the morning. I don't remember if we charged Henry for careless use of a firearm. Keep in mind that this is not uncommon. Every New Year's Eve you could hear people blasting shotguns and rifles from their porch. In the end, the gun was destroyed. One of the many that I would seize during my time in the community.

CHAPTER 6

Please, listen to me.

It was a call of a break and enter in progress. The suspect had gained entry to the house via breaking the windows. I was the first one dispatched to the complaint and rushed to the address. I came on scene to observe several windows in the duplex shattered. At this point, I should have waited for back up—rookie mistake—but with my side arm out, I entered the home announcing, "Police!" The home had been destroyed with furniture thrown all over the place. I immediately thought to myself that I knew the layout of this style of duplex. A friend I had growing up had lived in a duplex exactly like this. I cleared the bottom floor first; checking closets, the kitchen, etc. Then, I proceeded upstairs where the lights were off. Someone easily could have pegged me off as I walked upstairs and there would be nothing my flashlight or 9mm Smith & Wesson sidearm could have done. They had a tactical advantage.

I entered the first room at the top of the stairs and noticed the suspect laying face down on the bed, like he passed out. With my sidearm pointed at the suspect, I gave the command, "Police, you're under arrest, let me see your hands". It was at this point my partner rushed up behind me and said I should have waited for him. I was still on recruit field training. We had a good discussion afterwards, and I realized the dangerous situation I just put myself in. We were able to wake the suspect and handcuff him, gave him a quick search and brought him outside.

It was outside that everything took a sudden turn, the owner of the house came home from a local dance with her child in a stroller and said, "That's my husband." It turns out the "suspect" was intoxicated and locked himself out of the home. So, he just busted all the windows to gain entry. The complainant, understandably, saw this as a break and enter and reported it to police. Well, the handcuffs came off the suspect at this time and we proceeded to take details from everyone: name, date of birth, etc. It was in this discussion that the wife informed us that in fact a fight had occurred at the local dance between her and her husband. The husband, at one point, had assaulted the wife. So, back in cuffs he went, and this time for assault. He was searched again and brought to the detachment by my partner.

I stayed with the wife and her child. The child must have been about eight months old and was strapped in a blue stroller. I went back into the home and spoke with the wife. I begged her several times to let me bring her and her child to a women's shelter in the neighboring town, but she wouldn't let me. I had such a bad feeling in my stomach that this was something I was supposed to do.

There was nothing I could do to change her mind, so I did the next best thing I could do. I helped clean up and board up the windows the best I could with cardboard. After that was done, I said goodbye and left to finish the rest of the night shift.

It was about noon the next day that I was woken up by my partner's sirens next door as he raced out of his residence. What the hell was going on, I thought. It was shortly after this that I was called back to work. The lady that I tried to get to a shelter had been murdered. Murdered upstairs while her child was still in the blue stroller downstairs.

I was immediately hit with a sense of grief, like this was my fault. I now know this is called "survivors' guilt." I had begged this woman to let me take her to a place where she would be safe, but she did not listen. I did everything that I could to protect this woman and I failed. I lived with these feelings for a long time and had thoughts about this poor child hearing her mother being murdered. Why didn't she just listen to me? I also thought I was going to be in a lot of trouble. I was the last person to see her and I didn't do my job.

My job was to serve and protect, and I failed.

In the end, a suspect was located and tried for murder.

The guilt from this file still lives with me.

CHAPTER 7

Up in flames

It was another night shift when the call came in. There was a house on fire just down the road from the detachment. The jail guard and I went and looked outside and saw the flames. The jail guard started running towards the house saying that it was his uncle's. I told him to hold on as he was watching prisoners. The volunteer fire department was enroute to put out the fire. Everyone was accounted for except one person, the uncle. The fire department was able to put out the fire after some time and police held containment overnight until we could search the debris in the morning.

Morning eventually came and three of us attended. Community members surrounded the house as we walked into the debris where we located the uncle. He was near the door but couldn't make it out. It looked like he tried and he had come close but he must have suffocated in the smoke. All that was left of him was a torso and a head. The arms and legs were burnt off. The only way I could process what I was seeing was by saying to myself, "This smells like barbecue." And it did. People are not meant to see this kind of stuff, but I did. We carried the body out of the house and placed it in a body bag. The body was then escorted to the nursing station and kept in the cooler until arrangements were made by the coroner. That smell of burning flesh never left me. It makes me sick to think that my mind takes me to the point of saying what I did to myself, but I guess that's how the mind works when trying to process stuff like this. Family surrounding us and crying, while we are in a pit digging out a smoking body. What's normal about that? Nothing.

Chapter 8

Gas sniffers

Sadly, as mentioned before, addiction can affect anyone. Children, I found out, are no different. The high of choice was gasoline. Children would steal jerry cans of fuel from the community and would go and sniff gasoline to get high.

One nightshift, I was dispatched to a complaint of children who were high inside of a residence. My backup member and I attended a well-known trailer in the community and gained entry to the residence. Upon entry, I was immediately slapped in the face with the stench of gasoline. It was so strong that it smelled like you were at the gas station fuelling up your vehicle and splashed some on yourself. We found at least three kids high out of their tree on gasoline. It was sad to see. At one point, I went back out to my police vehicle. I can't remember what I was looking for, but when I returned to the trailer to go help my partner with the kids, he asked me, "Where the hell have you been? You've been gone for half an hour." I have no recollection of how long I was outside for. It might have been 30 minutes. I don't remember. I was probably high on gas fumes. I can remember that we called Child and Family Services to come and deal with the kids, seized the jerry cans, drove to the nursing station to get checked out, and filled in a hazardous occurrence report. It's safe to say that I lost a few brain cells that night. This would be the first of two occurrences in my career where I unintentionally got high on gas fumes.

Chapter 9

You're my backup?

I enjoyed my time in the communities I was first stationed at. I was a go-getter And I didn't like to sit around in the office. I enjoyed trying to find impaired drivers and pulling people over. In the detachment, there was a clip board of people on outstanding warrants. It wasn't hard to find these people; you just had to go to their house and knock on the door and arrest them. It was simple, but a task where it appeared that most officers in the smaller detachment area didn't want to do. Well, I got there and off I went, clearing up warrants. I was only in the office when I had paperwork to do. Some of the people in the community were not used to this. They were used to the police members staying in the office and just responding to the calls.

One night, I was conducting an impaired investigation after I came across a vehicle that was in the ditch outside of the home. As I was talking with the driver, a female came out of the home and started to interfere with the investigation. I warned her that she could be arrested for obstruction and she didn't listen. This time I used my "police voice," which we were taught in basic training. It was used to control the scene with an affirmative voice. So, I used my affirmative voice and instructed the female to get back into the house, to which she listened and I continued my investigation.

The next night my two backup members called me into the office to talk to me. They told me that I just go around screaming at people and that people were planning to attack me when I was off duty. I didn't take this very lightly and asked them who it was, to which they wouldn't tell me. This really pissed me off and I became fearful for my personal safety.

The chief of police was advised, but nothing was done. I began sleeping with my handgun by my nightstand and answering the door to my home with my gun hidden behind the door. It was common for people to come knock on the door of your personal residence to make complaints at all hours of the day or night.

It was at this point that I knew I couldn't trust my backup officers and knew that they were mad because I was making them look bad.

This same theme again happened at another complaint when a suspect was being arrested and I took charge. The suspect had been laying down on his bed and I was the only one struggling to get him under control while my backup officer was standing in the doorway watching me.

I never did trust those three members again.

Chapter 10

Out of gas

I can remember a lot about this call, including how the weather was, what I was doing, and what happened at the end of it. I was in one of the neighbouring communities serving subpoenas when the call came in. Two females had flipped their car over the bridge and an infant had been in the car as well. I was already 40 minutes away from the detachment and the occurrence address was another 40-odd minute from there. There I was, the lone police officer in charge of this complaint until backup could come and help me. With lights and sirens blazing, I headed down the dirt road as fast as I could to get to the next community. While enroute, I was updated that all parties had been taken out of the vehicle and an air ambulance had taken the infant to the hospital in a bigger centre. After a lengthy journey, I finally reached the nursing station in the community only to find utter chaos upon my arrival. Earlier, I had passed by the accident scene to secure it. At the nursing station, I encountered community members gathered around two deceased females on stretchers in the lobby.

With back up on the way to help me out, I began the investigation by taking statements from who I could and the process of identifying the deceased. It felt like an eternity that I was out there by myself. It was at least one and a half hours before my backup arrived. I continued to update my supervisor as to the ongoing investigation, as I sought guidance when needed.

My supervisor and several other members arrived on scene later in the afternoon and we finished our investigation on scene.

It was then time to transport the bodies from the community to the coroner who would take them from there. Up where I was, there was no such thing as the coroner coming and transporting the bodies. The police did this.

We toe-tagged the females and placed them in body bags.

I was driving a Chevrolet Tahoe and placed one body in the backseat of my vehicle. While my sergeant—sarge for short—was driving a Chevrolet Suburban and placed a body in the back of his. The convoy of police and victim services departed the community by means of a forestry road. Sarge was in front; I was in the middle while victim services and their truck was behind me. It was an odd scene driving with a body in the rear-view mirror of my vehicle. Needless to say, I turned the air conditioning on to the rear part of the vehicle to try and keep the body as cool as I could.

These roads were bush roads: narrow, bumpy, and at one point went through a patch of swamp on either side. At one point, I witnessed sarge go off the road to the right, getting stuck in the swamp. During this process a tree limb was kicked up and hit both rear doors of the suburban.

Well, sarge gets out and started to panic. We were in the middle of nowhere and his vehicle was stuck in a swamp with a body inside of it. He was worried that people would see us stuck on the side of the road with the bodies. So, he got out and tried to open the door to get the body out. The plan was to put the body that he was transporting into the truck box of the victim services unit. The truck box had a canopy on it, so it wasn't going to be like, putting a dead person into the truck box like an old couch and keep going. the sarge tried to open the doors and they didn't open. The tree limb that hit the doors was just in the right angle to jam them shut.

Along came another constable with a crowbar and he tried to open the doors without any luck. Well, shit, at this point old sarge was really starting to panic. Then it was my turn. I gave it the old heave-ho and I slipped ass over tea kettle into the swamp.

It was funny as hell and gave us the laugh we needed in this stressful situation. I was soaking wet and full of swamp water. Sarge was now in full panic. The only choice left was to bust the rear windows on the suburban and have someone climb in and pass the body out through the window. So, sarge grabbed his baton and smashed the window. Someone got in the back and passed the body through the window and we loaded her into the truck box of the victim services unit. Victim services then took off to meet the coroner while I stayed behind for a bit to see if I could help get sarge's vehicle unstuck, but it was stuck good. We were about an hour and half away from the nearest tow truck, so sarge was going to have to wait for the tow truck to arrive. Off I went with my body.

Keep in mind that at the beginning of the shift I did not plan to head to the community that I did. I also did not plan on transporting a dead body in the rear of my police vehicle. One thing about policing is that you can always expect the unexpected, just like we did and what was about to come.

I made it about 30 minutes away from the community when I hit the gravel road off the dirt trail, about 40 minutes away from the detachment to meet the coroner. I also ran out of gas. So here I was, stuck on the side of the road in the blistering heat with no gas and no air conditioning in the vehicle. Holy shit, I thought to myself. What kind of gong show did this just turn into. I got on the radio and gave the chief of police a heads up that I needed someone to come meet me with some fuel. That took about half an hour and I just sat in my police vehicle, with no air conditioning and a dead body to talk to. Eventually someone did show up with fuel and I was able to meet the coroner for the body transition. Only in policing will you have stories like this.

After Falling in the Swamp

Chapter 11

The La Bamba plane

As a kid I had three favorite movies: Smokey and the Bandit, Cannonball Run, and La Bamba. In the movie La Bamba, at the end, Ritchie Vallens, Buddy Holly, and The Big Bopper died in a plane crash in Iowa. I remember that scene well and have the image of a small plane going up in the dark night never to be seen again.

Well, there were only two ways to get to the isolated community, either by small plane or driving the bush road. During the summer months, I mostly took the small plane and it immediately reminded me of La Bamba. It was a small, red and white Cessna and I just didn't trust it. Since it was a small plane, we would feel every little bit of turbulence.

There was one event in this airplane that will forever be etched in my mind. I was doing prisoner transport in the plane when the prisoner pointed to his door and said, "I think this is supposed to be locked!" I looked at the door and noticed that it was unlocked. I don't know how far up we were, but losing a handcuffed and shackled prisoner from the plane couldn't be good. I told the pilot and he told me to lock the door. The prisoner looked at me and laughed as a way to destress himself. I was a tad stressed!

Chapter 12

It's now a step side.

It was a call about a stolen quad last seen in the bush in the community. I grabbed my keys to the full-size police truck and off I went to make patrols. Eventually, I was able to pinpoint where the quad might have been and said to myself, "Ya, this truck can make it on the bush trail." So, there I went driving along the bush on the trail, but as I got further into the bush the trail became smaller and smaller. Eventually, branches started rubbing up against the truck and I came to a dead end. "Dammit," I said. I took a look back in the mirror and there was no way I was going to be able to back out of this one. The only way that I could get this truck out of the bush was to turn around and push over some trees with the truck. I started maneuvering the truck to turn it around. I could see the trees falling and could hear the crunching. I knew right then that I would have some explaining to do. I eventually turned the truck around after blazing a new path and made my way out of the bush. I parked and walked around my vehicle to check out the damage and I found a substantial amount. The entire truck was scratched and the truck box on the rear passenger side had been pushed in. It looked like one of those step-side trucks you would see in the 90s.

Honesty and integrity are key components to being a cop. If you don't have them, you shouldn't be a cop. I made my way back to the detachment and stopped at the residence of the chief of police and explained the situation. To my surprise, I didn't get in any heck for the event but rather got a pat on the back for being honest about what happened.

When I eventually transferred, the big joke was that I would take the pushed-in truck panel with me. Needless to say, I was cautious with my bush patrols after this. And I never did find that quad!

Chapter 13

Dogs

I love animals and always have. This next part of the job was absolutely brutal. In the small communities the police are called to deal with the dog complaints of stray dogs, aggressive dogs, etc. We even had to put them down at times, which I friggin hated and tried every time to get someone else to do it. Sadly, there are a couple times where I had to put down a dog and it broke my heart. The scenes from this will forever be etched in my mind.

The first one I remember was unexpected. Me and my partner were racing to a residence when a stray dog jumped in front of my truck. BAM, I hit it and underneath the truck it went. I stopped and verified that the dog was dead and threw it in the back of the truck box and continued on with the warrant execution. After we got the warrant executed, I had the task to find out what to do with the dog. I felt so bad and didn't think about the kilometers I could go and dump the body of the dog in the bush, but I didn't think of that. I remembered that back in the community there was an open dumpster at one of the local confectionaries. I didn't think it would be a problem if I dumped it in the dumpster, so I did. It was a day later that the detachment received a call from the store owner to report that a dog was in the dumpster. Once again, I fessed up to putting the dog in there as I didn't know what to do with it.

The second dog incident was even worse. I was in the isolated community at the time when we got a call from a homeowner saying that their dog was aggressive and not letting them out of the car. We arrived at the residence to find the dog on the porch and the family sitting in their car. The father requested that police shoot the dog. Dammit! My partner and I developed a plan. I would taser the dog on the porch and while the dog was subdued my partner would go up and shoot it with his pistol. I approached the porch and ZAP! Down the dog went. It squealed in pain from the taser and I wanted to cry. My partner then put one bullet in its skull and killed it. The next day my corporal got a thank you phone call from the homeowner and said that he wanted to thank the crying policeman. I don't remember tearing up but I must have been. To this day I can still hear that dog.

Several months passed by and another homeowner called police to come put down their dog as it bit a child. After talking with my supervisor, I brought some dog food with me. The plan was to dump the food on the ground and sneak up and shoot it.

I arrived at the residence and saw this husky-type dog and I opened the bag of food and dumped it on the ground. The dog, hungry, immediately began eating. I then came up behind him upset and put four rounds at close range in the back of its head. I was upset and wanted to make sure that the dog was dead so I reloaded four rounds into the shotgun and blasted it again. A total of 8 rounds were used. With the dirty deed done, I put the dog in the truck box and brought it to the landfill and disposed of it. The next day I went on days off.

While I was on days off, I received a phone call from my supervisor asking where I had put the dog's head. I told him it was in the dump. Turns out we had to keep the head for a rabies check as it bit a child. Well, I wasn't near the landfill and was on days off, so someone else had to go to the landfill, take the dog out and cut off its head. Sorry, my bad!

It wasn't all bad with dogs. As I had such a big heart for them, every time I would fly in I would bring dog food and milk bones to feed the strays. I was like the Pied Piper and would feed the dogs as I patrolled. I would have a trail of dogs following the police truck, and man that pissed off the chief of police but I didn't care.

We even had two strays that would hang around the detachment. One we called Yoyo, as he would bounce from members residences and the detachment all day. The other we called Paws, which was a talkative husky. When winter would hit, I would build shelters for Paws and Yoyo and even let them into my house to warm up, despite that I was told not to.

One night, I had to have a good laugh at myself. We got a call of a break and enter at the local maintenance shop. I was on call, so I suited up and had dispatch call out my backup. While enroute, my backup I made a plan to take the rear of the building while I would go to the front. I arrived on scene as quietly as I could, unholstered my pistol, and had it at the low ready and began walking the border of the front of the building. All of a sudden, I could hear some rustling coming from the wooden garbage bin. No way, I thought, I found them hiding in the garbage. I pointed my firearm at the garbage bin and as I did that, the lid of the bin popped off and out jumped a dog! I don't know where this next thing came from but I pointed my 9-mm sidearm at him and yelled, "Freeze." Freeze? Was this the Police Academy movie? I laughed out loud at my stupidity and my partner came around. The building was locked up and it was a false alarm.

Dogs Paws and Yoyo

Chapter 14

Patch over and time to move

It was August 9, 2009, and I finally made it. Years of trying to get into the RCMP and all my hard work had paid off. It was time to patch over from the Tribal Police to the Royal Canadian Mounted Police.

I had been a cop for three years so far, but I was so excited to jump ship into the RCMP. My ultimate dream had come true. I was sworn in that day at the RCMP detachment in Grande Prairie, Alberta. I was happy to sign my name on the dotted line, swearing to move anywhere in Canada and was willing to give my life for someone else's. I was disappointed in the fact that the RCMP didn't have a badge for me to carry yet, because it had been backordered or hadn't been made, and the only thing I had to prove that I was a cop was this form I just signed. Well, I also had an official RCMP identification card with no photo on it, so that was great. Little did I know that this clusterfuck was going to continue when I arrived at my first posting in Northern British Columbia.

My first fiancée, my step son, and I arrived, and I was stunned by the beauty of it all. The mountains, the Indigenous art, and the ultimate prize was that there was a road coming in and out of the community. I could drive somewhere on my day off. That was awesome. I arrived at the detachment and met one of my coworkers and he showed us to our barracks. It was a nice, three-level home, perfect for the three of us and my two cats. It took us a little while to settle in, but it was worth it.

Not to my surprise, I spent my first shift in the RCMP in a pair of jeans and borrowed uniform kit from other off-duty constables as I had nothing to use of my own. Everything down to the firearm was borrowed. Here we go again, I thought to myself.

I spent two years in this community and little did I know that when I got there this was going to be the beginning of the end. As mentioned before, this is where my wheels started to fall off and I started to notice changes in myself. At the end of my tour of duty in my first post with the RCMP, I ended up alone, being a new dad but without access to my child. The story of my mental health deteriorating had begun.

Now a member of the RCMP in my Scarlet Tunic

Chapter 15

Chili

It was near the end of my dayshift and I had just come home from a call when we got another one coming in. This time, a male was wanting to kill himself. Another suicidal male, I thought. I had already taken off all my gear and had been ready to relax, but it was time to get back out there. I put on my gear again and headed out the door.

The address wasn't too far from my residence, so I arrived on scene quite quickly. I immediately went to the front door of the residence and tried to open it, but it was locked. I then ran to the rear of the residence to see if that door was open before I started kicking doors in. There was a small window beside the door that I could look into. I could see the person had hung himself and was swaying back and forth and side to side. I updated my backup who was on their way and about 15 minutes out. "He's hanging in the basement and swinging," I said on the radio to my backup. I don't know why I remember that but that phrase has stuck with me. It was time to gain entry to the house. With one strong kick to the door, it flung open and that's when I confirmed that we had a problem on our hands. I ran up to the male who was still swinging. I lifted him up with one arm and managed to untie him. He fell to the ground and on the way down had hit his head on the freezer. With the lifeless body now lying on his back, I looked around and saw a plastic grocery bag beside him. I had no other barriers to protect myself while I was about to conduct CPR (cardiopulmonary resuscitation). I placed the bag over his mouth, poked a hole, and started. I will never forget the clanging of our teeth when they touched and the taste of chili that came into my mouth. As I went through the motions of CPR, backup arrived on scene but it was not the police. Locals from the community started to barge into the basement, as they had heard everything on the police scanner. Great, I thought to myself, not only do I now have to maintain CPR—which I was starting to get tired of—I now had to deal with people who were frantic about the situation going on. And from my experience with doing next of kin notifications, you can never tell how someone will react. My brain was also now trying to deal with the fact that one of these ten other people surrounding me could snap at any moment. Luckily, medical staff from the nursing station arrived and took over CPR. I was exhausted. It was only then that my coworkers arrived on scene. I tried my best to save this man as we worked on him for 30 minutes before a nurse called the doctor who pronounced him deceased. Again, I felt a lot of guilt over this. Could I have been faster putting my gear on and heading out the door? I remember that I had been annoyed that I just took off my gear when the call came in and I had to suit up again. The feeling of guilt still resides with me to this day.

Chapter 16

Machete

On a good day traveling between the detachment and the neighbouring community, it was at least 20 minutes away from me. The roads were narrow winding mountain roads, so you could not travel very fast even if you had your red and blues on. I remember it was around 4:30 a.m. and I was off call at 5 a.m.; so of course, a complaint would come in. I was awake anyway. I could never sleep when I was on call. Information provided to me from police dispatch was that a male was intoxicated and assaulted someone in a residence. Further information was provided that the occupants of the house were all locked in a room as they were afraid. Into the closet I went, like Superman in a phone booth to gear up. With my uniform back on and dispatch calling my backup who was 20 minutes away, off I went. I didn't know what kind of shit show I was about to get into on my own. The last time I got called to a shit show in the community, I had to argue with a guy who was stabbed. With a 20-minute head start on my backup, I headed out the door. I arrived on scene, and as it was about 5 a.m., I pressed the request-to-talk button on the radio to let dispatch know that I arrived while I exited my vehicle. The first thing I noticed was that it was really quiet. The entire community was quiet. No 5 a.m. parties going on, no birds chirping, nothing. I approached the white house, and opened the front door with my gun out. Again, quiet. So quiet you could hear a pin drop. I snuck up the stairs with my pistol at the low ready position and cleared the kitchen area. Nothing to be seen or heard there. I then backtracked and proceeded around the corner to find my suspect with half his torso leaning out of the bathroom. I had a choice at that moment and was about to proceed to arrest him when a loud voice in my head went "STOP! Don't go down there Tim." I believe that this was the voice of my deceased grandma keeping me safe. Many times, on the way to dangerous calls, I would talk to her asking her to and ask her keep me safe. After hearing this, I stopped. I now had my gun pointed at the suspect and had no idea how things would turn out. One false move and I would have to take someone's life, which I did not want to do nor live with. With my pistol pointed at the suspect I advised him that he was under arrest. There we were in a stare down in the middle of the hallway. There're a lot of scenarios that could have happened here; the worst was someone possibly losing their life, including me. We stood there, just talking until my backup arrived. I wish I could remember what we said during that time. Once my backup arrived, we were able to talk the suspect out of the washroom and into handcuffs. With the suspect now taken out of the residence and secured in the back of the police vehicle, my partner began to search for the members of the family that were locked in a room, as I went to the hallway to see what had been going on in the bathroom. To my surprise, indeed I found a weapon. In fact, I found a large machete. The type you would bring on a jungle expedition. If I would not have listened to the voice in my head telling me to stop, things could have been a lot different that morning. I was lucky again, and was able to go home after my shift, uninjured.

Chapter 17

The switch

There is one person that I remember dealing with while in my time up north, it is Sean. When he was sober, he was nice, polite, and not a problem. But when he drank, it was like someone flipped a switch. I fought with this guy several times and had hugs and coffee on other occasions.

The first time Sean and I went at it was when there was a complaint that he was at his residence causing a disturbance, breaking furniture and such. He was also on conditions to keep the peace and be of good behavior and to not be under the influence of alcohol or drugs. He was drunk, causing a ruckus, and needed to go to jail. I was the only one on shift and off I went to his house. I arrived at the residence and advised dispatch to check on me in five minutes. I knocked on the door and Sean came out. I could tell that Sean was intoxicated, he reeked of liquor, had red bloodshot eyes, started to talk slurring his words, and was unsteady on his feet. I advised Sean that he was under arrest, and the fight was on from there. There wasn't much room to have a good scuffle as we were on the porch. I managed to push Sean up against the side of the house and tried to get a pair of handcuffs on him. Sean retaliated by trying to donkey kick my testicles, but he missed and got me in the perineum instead. I am thankful that he missed his shot, as this scenario would have played out a lot different if I got kicked in the nuts. The struggle continued. I was able to manage to get a pair of handcuffs on him, but the fight was not over yet. Sean was then able to tug on the handle of my 9mm handgun. Down to the ground we went, and the fight was done. With Sean under control and things calmed down, he was placed in the cruiser and taken to the detachment for a bail hearing to see if he was going to stay in custody until trial or not.

A few days later, Sean showed up at the detachment to apologize, and I invited him in for coffee. We chatted about his alcoholism and how it was affecting him and his family. We also started browsing the internet looking for potential jobs. Sean was grateful.

It must have been a couple weeks later that Sean and I were at it again. He was intoxicated and causing a disturbance in the middle of the street and someone had called him in. My partner and I were quick to locate Sean in the middle of the road yelling in front of a residence. "Sean, you're under arrest," I said in a firm voice. Sean didn't like being told that he was going to be going to jail again, and the fight was on. My partner and I tried to get him under control with as little force as possible, but all three of us transitioned to the ground and the struggle continued. At one point, a witness yelled out to us, "Hey, do you need help?" I contemplated saying yes as I was now starting to get tired in the struggle, but somehow, we were able to get him under control, handcuffs on, and in the back of the squad car.

Over my two years in the community, I had many run-ins with Sean, but there was another side of him—the sober, gentle side. The time had come when it was time for me to transfer out of the community. I forget what circumstances brought us together one morning. Nevertheless, he was sober and I was giving him a ride somewhere. I told Sean that I was transferring and going to be leaving. "I'm going to miss you." He always called me by a different name as he would get me confused with another cop that would deal with him in years prior. It didn't bother me and I never corrected him. It really didn't matter. I told him that I would miss him too. We arrived at our destination and I let him out of the car and I gave him a big hug goodbye. That was the last time I saw Sean and I always hoped for the better for him.

Chapter 18

Fight at Home Depot.

It was July 2011 and I had recently transferred to the larger centre on Vancouver Island. A complaint came in from dispatch about a road-rage incident between a male in his 40s and a male in his late 60s at the Home Depot. It was reported that fists had been exchanged and the aggressor, the younger male, had fled into the store, to the plumbing aisle to be exact. Police arrived on scene and spoke to the victim, who advised that he was punched by the suspect. I don't recall the exact wording or reasons why the road rage occurred, but a statement was taken by one of my coworkers, and myself and my other partner entered the store to apprehend the suspect.

I should mention that it was a Sunday morning after church and the store was packed! I remember walking to the plumbing aisle and observed the suspect kneeling down and pretending to be shopping for some items. I also remember that the suspect was, in fact, grabbing some sort of pipe, which made sense because of the aisle we were in.

"You're under arrest for assault," I advised the male. Of course, this was met with some passive resistance and the fight was on. Police were now in the middle of the aisle in a cage match with the suspect. I say cage match, because staff of the store proceeded to close the gates of the aisle to lock us in and keep the public out. So, there we were in the middle of the aisle on the floor trying to gain compliance of the suspect. My partner and I were both on top of him as he squirmed on the floor. "Give me your hands," I shouted to no effect. It was at this point I struck the suspect in the ribs with a closed fist, which also had no effect. The suspect then retaliated by kicking me in the perineum. Again, I was kicked in the perinium, the second time in my career. I then escalated my use of force with the suspect and I advised him that if he did not comply, he was going to get tasered. And by advising, I mean shouting, "STOP RESISTING OR YOU'RE GOING TO GET TASERED!" It was after this that my partner and I were able to gain control of the suspect and place some handcuffs on him. Staff opened up the aisle and we brought the suspect to our squad car.

You might be asking yourself, if the story started with three police officers but only two were fighting with the suspect, why is that? Well, during all the commotion my second back up partner could not hear the radio and our calls for help in the plumbing aisle. He only found out that we were having a scuffle as we walked the suspect past him at the front of the store. To this day, I still keep saying to my buddy he was busy with the greeter enjoying a hot dog.

Chapter 19

Spiderman

It was a typical complaint that I already knew what was going to happen. A person hadn't been seen in a while and there is a bad odor coming from his apartment. Let's call him Mark. I remembered Mark from times I dealt with him and the fact that he was usually seen on his motorized scooter on the bike trail giving police the bird as they drove by.

My partner and I arrived at the apartment building and after getting the keys to his apartment walked up the stairs to his unit. We knocked on the door to no avail. At this point, given the circumstances, we gained entry to the unit and just as I thought, Mark was dead. He had been dead for a while, too, as he looked melted on the floor with oils and fluids coming out of his body. Thankfully, a window had been left open, thus there were barely any flies in the room. If I can now have you picture what kind of view I had here. The entrance way was so small that there was no way to get around Mark because there were cabinets on both sides. Someone had to get to Mark's wallet by the window in the living room. Me being junior to my partner, I had to get over Mark somehow. Remember when you were a child and could branch yourself with the arms and legs in the hallway and climb? That's sort of what I had to do to get over Mark. I position myself with one leg to one side of the countertop and on the other side did the same. As I carefully began to scale over Mark, all I could think was, please don't fall, please don't fall. I scaled over his body that was melting on the floor and made it to the other side.

I grabbed Mark's wallet from his backpack that was by the open window and tossed it to my partner who had watched me Spiderman over the melted body. We called the coroner's office and funeral home to come and pick up the body. I remained in the living room until Mark was placed in a body bag and removed, as I wasn't going to be lucky twice if I tried to scale over him one more time.

Chapter 20

Gerald

It was about midnight when I saw him sitting there. He was outside the homeless shelter just sitting on a park bench. Gerald was his name. We all knew him as he was a heavy drinker and spent a lot of time in the jail cell block at the detachment. He drank so much that there had come a point where police were directed to bring him to the hospital to sober up, instead of the jail, for his own safety.

I had a big heart for the homeless. While on patrol, I would stop and talk to them like any human being should. That night, I drove past Gerald on the bench and headed to Tim Hortons to get hot chocolates for Gerald and I. With both of our drinks in hand, I returned to the homeless shelter and sat beside him. "Here Gerald," I said as I gave him his drink. I then asked him, "Gerald, why are you outside?" I was curious to know why he was freezing instead of being warm in the shelter. "I yell and have nightmares," he replied. "So, I come outside so I don't wake anyone up," he continued. I took a sip from my cup and said, "What are your nightmares about?" Gerald replied, "Residential schools."

It was from that point we just sat in silence, knowing that we both understood each other. I stayed until my drink was done and I went back on patrol while Gerald sat there, on the bench.

It was later in my retirement that I asked one of my former co-workers if Gerald was still around. That's when I found out that Gerald had died, and was no longer haunted by his nightmares.

Chapter 21

I'll hold your hand.

"City police for a man down complaint." It had been a quiet night on the radio until 3 a.m. when the complaint came in. I took the call and got up from my chair in the office and headed to the scene, which was a local trailer park.

It was quiet and dark when I arrived on scene. I immediately noticed a male in his 60s lying in the middle of the road with blood coming out from the back of his head. I updated my supervisor and he and other members were enroute. I didn't know at the time what I was dealing with. Was this man robbed or assaulted?

The amber hue from the streetlights lit up the asphalt enough that I could see, but yet it felt eerie. The man was breathing. I gave the man a cursory search, looking for other signs of trauma just like I was taught in my first-aid course. "Hello, it's the police," I told him in his ear with no response.

I could hear in the distance that back up was on its way along with an ambulance. I continued my search for trauma and I reached into his back pocket of his jeans to grab his wallet in hopes of finding some sort of identification. It was at this point, with the little strength he had, that he tried to keep me from taking his wallet. I told him it was the police and he would be alright and held his hand. He gripped my hand as hard as he could and he could not talk. I kept consoling him that it was the police and he would be okay. In his wallet I was able to find the identification of the victim.

With the ambulance now on scene, we put our now known victim on the stretcher, but he wouldn't let go of my hand. He was put into the ambulance and driven away. I noticed after that his broken glasses were left behind, so I grabbed them and later put them into an exhibit locker. A few days later I was able to speak to the man's son about his father's glasses. At that point, I was informed that the man had passed away and it was due to his fall. I recall, after hanging up the phone, of having tears come down my face as I sat in the police cruiser. I didn't understand at that point why I was having such an emotional reaction. Years later, I finally grasped the reasons behind my reactions, realizing they stemmed from my diagnosis with Post Traumatic Stress Disorder.

Chapter 22

The Depot Days

Basic training for the RCMP is in Regina where all RCMP members, for many years, have spent six months out of their lives training to become a Mountie. They also train police officers for other police forces. This is where I had fit in. I was amalgamated into an RCMP troop and sweated the same sweat and cried the same tears when warranted. During my time at Depot, I kept my family and friends informed how things were going by sending them emails when I could. Happily, I was able to find these in my email account.

Saturday, May 13, 2006
Subject: Week 1 of 24 is done!!!

Hey everyone;

Well, I am done my first week at DEPOT. It was quite the culture shock. It is going to take a little getting used to but it is going to be fun. The best way to describe it here so far would be, it's like college and it's also like being in the military. I am just going to have to get used to getting up at 5 a.m. and going to bed around 11 p.m.

Other than that, everything is going well. It will be fun once I get my uniform and learn how to march. That's about all I have to say for now,

Talk to you later,

Tim

23 WEEKS TO GO!!!
Sunday, May 21, 2006
Hello everyone;

Sorry if I have not been able to respond to some of your emails, but I will try to reply as soon as I can. Things out here at the RCMP Training Academy are going well. You get your bad days and you get your good. But for now, the majority of them are good. I am having fun.

Drill Class is a lot of fun. Needless to say, the Drill Corporal. has yelled "BEDARD!!!" quite a few times. I get so nervous when he asks me questions and then I give the wrong answer. For instance, he asked me the other day what my number was in rank... I said "27" which was the number I had last class, so I assumed it was the same one today; well it was supposed to be 22.... so he says, "Do you have to go back to you school BEDARD? Maybe we should count together...1...2....3...4..." and he goes on down the line counting people for me. It was pretty funny and it was hard not to laugh.

I shot at a firing range for the first time in my life today. I was so nervous. I had the pistol on the target and I was shaking like a leaf. I still hit the target but on the lower portion. But after a few rounds, I ended up getting it right in the middle of the target. The firing instructors really get along with me and are funny, they use me for examples or the butt of jokes. Since once upon a time, they policed back in my hometown, they familiarized themselves with me and joke around with me. So that's nice to have and takes the stress off. Even the sergeant yells, "Hey bro, how is it going?" and the other corporal and constable laugh and tell jokes about me such as, "Okay guys, you can either do this the wrong way or the BEDARD way." So, it's funny and we have a good time.

I went for my first patrol drive around Regina in a cadet car this week. Needless to say, it was fun. One thing is that it is really hot out here marching everywhere in the sun. Especially for me since my uniform is black.

Well, I guess I should go and polish my boots for drill class tomorrow, since I do not want to hear, "BEDARD, do you know how to polish boots?"

Tim
22 weeks to go!!!

Saturday, June 3, 2006
Subject: Weeks 3 and 4 out of 24 are done!!!

Hello everyone;

How time flies over here. I am already going to be starting Week 5. I can't believe it. Anyways, things over here are starting to get a little more difficult. However, drill and firearms are getting better, I think I only did 40 push ups in my last drill class and I actually hit the target...56 out of 60 was the score!!!!

Fitness class is really hard though. We went for a 1.5-mile run. It was not the run that was hard but everything in between. So, we started the run and 1/3 way through we stopped to do "planks" and push ups. Needless to say, I was getting sick. It was also difficult doing this while people were yelling at you to "GO HOME, WHY ARE YOU IN THE BACK OF THE LINE BEDARD. WEST JET HAS A TV ON THEIR PLANES AND WE WILL GLADLY BUY YOU A TICKET HOME" and other stuff like that. But it's all part of the game and it has its purpose. I just chose to ignore it and kept on going the best way that I could. When we finished the run, half of the troop went and ran up the stairs, 5 flights of them I do believe, while the other people stayed back and did "planks," push ups and other exercises. When we were done on the stairs it was my group's turn to do the exercises. I did them the best that I could and I was feeling sick again all while listening to the instructors yelling at me. It was difficult, but I made my way through it. I am assuming that for the next 5 months all the gym classes are going to be like that. I am not looking forward to it, but it is all part of the game out here, and I will give it all I got. It has its purpose, because when I am going to be done training and out in the real world, I may be wrestling with someone by myself, in the middle of nowhere, who is trying to make sure I don't make it home that night. So as difficult as fitness class is going to be, I will give it 100% and not give up.

Other than fitness class, things are going well. The majority of the stuff I am learning right now was already covered during my time at MacEwan. So, it's nice not to be stressed and take it more as a review. Also, this allows me to have more time to concentrate on other stuff. There is also a lot of new stuff that I have been introduced to, so that takes the majority of my time to comprehend. Prince Edward also came to Depot on Friday and he was supposed to come and drop in on the class. Unfortunately, he did not, and I did not have the chance to meet him.

Well, I guess I should go and try to catch up on homework and I will talk to you all later.

Tim

Date: Sunday, June 25, 2006
Subject: Week 7 of 24 is done!!!

Hello everyone;

Sorry for not keeping you all updated in a while, but I will try my best. Things here at Depot have been going really well. I am getting into great shape and fitness class is getting better. The one thing that I find is that there are not enough hours in the day to get stuff done around here.
Even on the weekends it's... go, go, go.

Other than that, things are going well. I get O.C. "pepper" sprayed tomorrow, so I am not looking forward to that. I had defensive tactics, firearms and driving exams last week, which I passed. However, there are some key points that I need to improve on. I hope you all are enjoying your summer and I will try to update you all more often.

Tim

Date: Sunday, July 2, 2006
Subject: Week 8 of 24 is done

Hello everyone;

Well Week 8 is finally behind me and I am glad. It started out hot, really hot, since I got pepper sprayed. I was pepper sprayed last year around this time and I knew what was coming. So, I guess

I was able to control myself better this time around... but it still was the worst pain I had ever felt.

The rest of the week went pretty well, we actually earned the right to wear our boots. This was due to the fact that we had a great noon parade on Friday. Things are still going good out here and week nine is right around the corner. I can't wait until the halfway mark so I can actually start counting down the weeks instead of counting how many I have done.

I hope you all are enjoying your summer.

Tim

Date: Sunday, July 16, 2006
Subject: Week 11 of 24 done
Hello everyone;
Well Week 11 is finally done and over with. This week was pretty demanding with fitness class, police defense tactics and morning parades. We did a lot of striking this week in police defence tactics and on Thursday we had our "rings" boxing match. Well, it turned out that my match was the longest one out of the group at a little over 3 minutes. We were told it would only be for approximately 90 seconds. Needless to say, 30 minutes after the fight, my neck was starting to hurt and I was told I was slurring my words like I was intoxicated. I guess I also received a few good shots or two to the head because the doctor told me I had a slight concussion. I was then ordered to stay in the Medical Treatment Center for the rest of the afternoon.

That's all the news for me. Thank you everyone for your replies.

Talk to you later,
Tim

Date: Monday, July 31, 2006
Subject: Week 12 of 24 is done.
Hello everyone;

Week 12 is finally done and Week 13 has started. It was quite the busy week here at Depot with our first detachments. We responded to calls and dealt with the whole process from start to finish. It was really fun and was also quite the learning experience. I can't believe that I am halfway done with Depot and I have my midterm exam coming up this Thursday.

Tomorrow, we have our uniform run. This consists of us dressing up in our full duty gear and going running for an entire gym class. I am really starting to like gym class now... now that I am getting into good shape. I am not going to say that I am the best runner.... not by a long shot, but I can say that I am not running in the back of the pack anymore.

Anyways, I hope you all enjoy your week and I will talk to you later,

Tim

12 WEEKS 2 GO!!!

Date: Saturday, August 5, 2006
Subject: Week 13 of 24 Done
Hello everyone;

What a week it has been. It started out quite well with a uniform run. Basically, we put on all of our gear, including our soft body armour, and did our fitness class. We climbed ropes, did sprints, pull ups, sit ups and dreaded planks, all before we even got to the hard part. Once we eventually reached the baseball diamond, we then had to run to the fence and back before picking up our partner for a "fireman" carry. I carried my partner a quarter of the way to where we had to drop him and then had to crawl in the grass using our elbows. It was very similar to what you see in army movies. Once we finished that, we sprinted back to the gym and we were finally done. It was a hard class, but fun to do.

I also had my midterm this week. I am proud to say that I received a superior rating with an 82%. I also managed to put another "gem" into my Depot archives. This one happened on noon parade on Monday.

Since we were on a noon parade with a graduating troop, the training officer of Depot was there inspecting all of the troops. It also happened that our drill constable was also on parade and in the process of inspecting us before the training officer did.

Reference, about 8 weeks prior, I kept calling our drill constable, corporal. At the time, I got told, "I did not know you could promote me, Cadet BEDARD." Anyways, here is how the noon parade played out...

Corporal: How are you today, Cadet BEDARD?

ME: I did not say anything for some reason.

Corporal: Cadet BEDARD, that was a question. How are you today?

ME: Sorry corporal, I am doing good today, and yourself?

(At this point the Corporal slowly starts walking away and talking to me at the same time.)

Corporal: When the training officer comes by, make sure you call him Sir.

ME: Yes Sir, I will do that..." At this point, I referenced myself to 8 weeks prior when I was calling the drill constable.... a corporal. Only now, I demoted him this time and called him Sir. I figured I was really going to hear about this one.

Corporal: He turns around and smiles at me and says, "You know what BEDARD, this is why you're my favorite!"

I thought this was quite funny. This is coming from the constable. For some reason, I don't call him by his proper rank and has told me that I look like I am doing some sort of flamingo dance, asked me if it was Halloween because it looked like I was bobbing for apples, and other funny quirks because of my marching.

Well, that's all the fun I had this week. Next week, we get our dorms inspected by the training officer of Depot and also go for our B.O.L.O. "Be on the lookout" drive in Regina... another test!!!

I hope you all are having a great summer.

Talk to you later,

Tim

11 Weeks to Go

Date: Sunday, August 20, 2006
Subject: Week 15 of 24 is done!!!
Hello everyone;

Well, Week 15 is done and out of the way. Things out here are still going well and I am anxious to be finished.... another 9 weeks to go.

I was tear gassed last Tuesday, and it turned out not to be that bad. And I also had a few other tests. The weeks are really starting to fly by now and I cannot believe that I am going into Week 16. I shall keep you all updated... talk to you later, Tim

Date: Sunday, August 27, 2006
Subject: Week 16 of 24 Done!!
Hello everyone;

Well Week 16 of Depot is finally done and what a week it has been.

Monday was a lot of fun. It consisted of driving down the highway, trying out a bunch of fun maneuvers and doing "cop turns" on a gravel road.

Basically, the whole time I was driving it felt like I should be getting a ticket, but yet, there was a cop next to me in the passenger seat telling me to drive like this!!! It was a lot of fun and by far the best day I had at Depot yet.

This week we also earned the right to wear our pants with stripes on them. Tomorrow we also start our 2nd detachments and we will be doing impaired scenarios. So, we are going to go through the steps of what to do with an impaired driver and how to approach these situations safely.

I only have 57 days left in Depot and I can't wait to be done, but on the other hand, I think I am going to miss all the fun times I had here so far.

Have a good week and talk to you again next Sunday,
Tim
57 DAYS TO GO!!!!

Driving around Regina Saskatchewan practicing my skills

Date: Sunday, September 3, 2006
Subject: Week 17 of 24 is Done!!!

Hello everyone;

Well Week 17 is done and I am glad. The beginning of the week was not going so well, it seemed like everything I was doing was going wrong, no matter what I did. Things started to get better as the week went by. I ended up doing my first impaired scenario where I got called to a complaint of a female passed out in her vehicle. So, I went through the steps as I would in real life, and now I am still doing the paperwork as I would in real life... lol.

I also had my 2nd detachment this week and I got called to an alarm complaint at a store, which then turned out to be a break and enter. It was quite the learning experience needless to say.

Today I am still playing catch up and I have 3 files to complete by tomorrow morning, so it might be a late night for me tonight.

This coming week should be fun, considering we have 2 days of track; which involves racing around an obstacle course in a cop car with lights and sirens going. It should be a blast.

I hope you all enjoy the week,

Tim
50 days to GO!!!!

Date: Sunday, September 10, 2006
Subject: Week 18 of 24 is done!!!

Hello everyone;

Well week number eighteen is done and I could not be happier. As of today, I only have 43 days left here until I am officially a police officer, I can't wait.

This week has been a lot of fun. It started with 2 days of racing around a track. We got to apply different driving maneuvers at different speeds and some people had the chance to get more confident behind the wheel. If you can imagine what it was like going around on a go-kart track, it basically was the same, but we used a full-sized car and travelled at speed up to 100 km/h. It was a blast.

Today I also participated in the memorial parade for the fallen RCMP officers at Depot. It was really nice to see and it was an honour to participate in. Plus, while we were being inspected on parade, the COMMISSIONER of the RCMP, *Commissioner Zaccardelli*, came and talked to me. It was surely a day to remember.

Well, I shall talk to you all later,
Tim
43 DAYS LEFT!!!!!

Date: Sunday, September 24, 2006
Subject: Week 20 of 24 is done!!!

Hello everyone;

Sorry I did not have the time to email you all last Sunday. It's starting to get really busy around here with finals and such. I only have a few weeks left at Depot and I can't wait.

The tests are starting to come in. I had my pistol qualifications last week and I had my best shooting day since I got here. I shot a 225 out of 250, which earned me the right to get my Cross Pistols patch on my ceremonial uniform. This week I have to qualify on the shotgun and I also have my police defense tactics final It should go alright.

Sorry for the short email; once again it's going to be a late night of homework. Have a good week and I shall talk to you all next Sunday.

Tim

Saturday, September 30, 2006
Subject: Week 21 of 24 is Done!!!!

Hello everyone;

Well Week 21 is finally done and I am another week closer to accomplishing my goal. It was a busy week for me with a lot of running around. I had my shotgun qualifications to do and my Police Defence Tactics Exam... which I passed.

This week we also had a Canadian celebrity on the base. Rick MERCER from the show on CBC, *Rick Mercer's Monday Report*, was here. He was with a couple of troops for the day going through various Depot experiences. It should be fun to watch once it hits the air. Unfortunately, he did not show up with our troop.

My written final exam is going to be this week and it is going to be nice to get that out of the way. Well, that's all the news for me and I will talk to you all later.

Tim

Date: Monday, October 9, 2006
Subject: Week 22 of 24 Done!!!

Hello everyone;

Well week number 22 is finally done and I cannot be any happier. It was a busy week for me with finals and Police Defence Tactics benchmarks; but I passed. So now I have to pass my final detachment which is tomorrow. After that, I will have a few little things to do but the majority of the exams will be done.

It is starting to get a little colder out here and I am glad that I came to Depot when I did. Well, I shall keep you all updated and thank you for the emails. Talk to you later.

Tim

2 weeks to go!!!

Friday, November 10, 2006
Subject: Depot is all done and I just finished my first set of shifts.

Hello everyone;

Sorry about the delay in the usual update, I have been quite busy since the last time I talked to you all.

So, I finally reached one of my goals, to graduate from Depot. I accomplished this on Oct. 23rd and I have to thank all of you for your support. Your emails helped a lot, especially when the days were going bad; it was nice to know that I had friends and family supporting me.

Depot was quite the experience, it pushed me to my limits and challenged them. It's funny, the night of grad was happy and it was sad at the same time. I had made such great friends at Depot and had so much fun, that in a way, I did not want to leave. During the summer at Depot, I had the chance to meet the commissioner of the RCMP, meet Rick MERCER from CBC and almost meet the prime minister and the prince. So now where am I?

Well, I am now a constable with the Tribal Police and my girlfriend and I are settled in a duplex in the community. I am working side by side with the RCMP out of the brand-new detachment here. I go on the same calls as them and use just about all of their equipment. It is quite a big detachment area and is full of beautiful scenery. The people out here are great and it is going to be a great experience. My girlfriend is also looking around town for a full-time job, currently she is working at a confectionery. I also plan on getting my degree in criminal justice through Athabasca University once I get the feel of the new job.

Thank you once again everyone for supporting me throughout my time at Depot and supporting me throughout the years to help me achieve my goal. Thank you all once again and keep me updated on how you all are doing.

Tim

Conclusion

As I write this paragraph, it has been ten years since my last traumatic incident in uniform and it still feels like yesterday. A lot has happened in those ten years and I am still not the same person that I was, and I will never be the same. I will forever be on medication to aid with the flashbacks, anxiety, and depression. I will always be under the care of a psychologist as well. I've dealt with addiction to numb the pain and help me disconnect from my reality. On a positive note, two years ago I was introduced to one of my best friends. She goes by the name of Hazel. She is my service dog that I acquired from Vancouver Island Compassion Dogs in Qualicum Beach, British Columbia. She is by my side everywhere I go, and especially loves going to the gym. She's changed my life for the better. I still have a lot of work to do but with Hazel by my side, it's a little bit easier.

I wrote this book in order to help those who think that they are alone. I also wrote this book to help those understand what it is like to deal with the demons that come with the job from serving your country. There is a lot of work still to be done to get rid of the stigma and old-school mentality that comes with opening up about your mental health, but with steps like this, a small portion of that is able to be healed.

Tim Bedard

Hazel and I

Hazel my Service Dog

2009 in Beautiful British Columbia

www.ingramcontent.com/pod-product-compliance
Lightning Source LLC
LaVergne TN
LVHW041536060526
838200LV00037B/1012